Let us Praise the Lord.

Poetry by Geraldine Craw

Copyright 2022 Geraldine Craw

Published by Wild Strawberries Publishing, New Zealand.

www.wildstrawberriespublishing.co.nz

Cover art by Geraldine Craw

All rights reserved. No part of this publication may be reproduced or transmitted in any form or by any means, electronic, mechanical, digital, photocopying, recording or otherwise, or stored in a retrieval system, without written permission of the copyright owner.

ISBN: 978-0-473-66346-9

"Scripture quotations taken from the (NASB®) New American Standard Bible®, Copyright © 1960, 1971, 1977 by The Lockman Foundation. Used by permission. All rights reserved. www.lockman.org"

Let us praise the Lord from one generation to another.

What is Christian poetry

If not a touch from the heart of God

To be shared with others?

Introduction

My heart is, that those who love the Lord God and His son, Jesus Christ, will never stop seeking Him. That we will never stop longing for the touch of His glory to fill our lives. That as the deer pants for water, so we too will thirst for the Living God. (Ps 42.1). Psalm 22.3 tells us that God dwells in the praises of his people. What a place to meet with Him. As we lift our voices in praise and thanksgiving, the Holy One, the Creator of the universe, comes and meets with us.

Matthew 5.8 states, the pure in heart shall see God. My prayer is that we will come to the feet of Jesus in meekness and contrition, and continually pour out our love for Him. I hope the poems in this book will be an encouragement to the follower of Christ (or encourage others to find this amazing life in Christ) in this modern-day world. For those who would clean their hands and their hearts ready to ascend the hill of the Lord with praise and thanksgiving, I pray you gain joy from this book.

And for those who love colouring; the Lord has given us an amazing playground full of colour. Feel free to fill this book with your colours. – Geraldine Craw 2022.

Contents:

Love the Lord our God	7
Praise	9
In poetry	11
Light a Fire	13
In Praise	15
Shanty Paddock	17
Your Presence	19
More than Pretty	21
Thin Place	23
My Heart	25
Let our Hands reach out	27
First Love	29
Kiss of Air	31
A Place of Wonder	33
I will Praise You	35
Poem inspired by Psalm 118	37
A Dark Place	39
Light	41
Storms and Battles	43
Soaring	45
Wide place	47
The Veil	49
A place of Rolling Hills	51
Touched	53
Camp Fire	55

Taste of Heaven	57
Your Love, Whispered	59
Floating in the Words of a Psalm	61
Sit at the Feet of Jesus	63
Even in Winter	65
A Hiding Place	67
Sing in the Hills	69
You are Here	71
Can I Praise You?	73
A Painted Sky	75
At the End	77

Observations:

Ferns	8
Tiny Ripples	36

Psalms used throughout the book:

Psalm 145

Psalm 84

Psalm 138

Psalm 147

About the Author	78

Love the Lord our God.

Let the inner-most parts of our being
Rise up in praise and love
For the Lord our God.

May we bring forth goodness
And walk in never-ending wells of gratefulness
As we thank and worship Jesus.

Ride an effervescent flood of song
Drawn from the deepest recesses of our heart
To honour and adore Him
When we fall to our knees.

Let the words of our mouth
Carry us through the veil
Into the throne room of grace
To meet with and glorify the Lord our God.

We cry out and surrender the deepest wave of love,
With all our heart, with all our mind
And all our strength.
Let our praise burst forth
And bless the King of Creation,
Always.

Ferns
dangle
From the
River bank.
A miniature garden,
A tiny ecosystem,
Created by the Lord God.

Praise

I will praise You, my Lord God
All the length of my days.
I will tell the next generation
Of Your goodness.
I will speak out my love, forever.
May You be praised.

May You be praised, my God
In the folds of the hills
That hide secret valleys.

May You be praised, my Lord,
On the tops of mountains
That open to the heavens.

May You be praised,
By the words of my mouth,
and the writings of my pen.
May You always be praised.

I will extol Thee, my God, O King;
And I will bless Thy name forever and ever,
Every day I will bless Thee,
And I will praise Thy name forever and ever.

Psalm 145: 1-2

In Poetry

In poetry

I touch the hand of the Almighty.

With words of praise and thanksgiving

I push through

Into the eternal.

Stretch out open hands, open heart,

Step through to

Another world

Another love.

Face uplifted,

Face rejoicing,

Heart overflowing.

Touched.

Touched by

Love inexpressible

A love so wonderful,

Mercy giving.

Peace and kindness

Falls around me,

About me.

It washes over me.

Great is the Lord,
And highly to be praised;
And His greatness is unsearchable.
One generation shall praise Thy works to another,
And shall declare Thy mighty acts.
Psalm 145: 3-4

Light a Fire

I would like to speak with Christian Poetry.
To light a fire
That spreads out and abroad.
Declaring the beauty of the Lord Jesus.

Oh Lord, I praise You
Oh Lord God, I love You.
You have given me
Times of worship
And praise
In Your presence.
So wonderful.

I am grateful
To live in a green land
Under today's blue-white garden sky.

Then four dogs bark,
And say,
Let's go.

On the glorious splendour of Thy majesty,
And on Thy wonderful works
I will meditate.
And men shall speak of the power of Thine awesome acts;
And I will tell of Thy greatness.
Psalm 145: 5-6

In Praise

In praise
I lift my hands,
Lift my voice to the Lord God.

My heart,
My being longs to see You,
But none can behold the face of God
And live.
Let Him hide me in the secret place,
In the cleft of the rock
As He passes by.

I wait on bended knees,
In a hidden room.

They shall eagerly utter
The memory of Thine abundant goodness,
And shall shout joyfully
Of Thy righteousness.

Psalm 145: 7

Shanty Paddock

The paddock is bare today
Of its four-footed creatures
That usually graze this habitat.
The hill curves above me
Stark and green, against a blue
End-of-winter sky.
Grasses
Soak in warmth and sun,
To refresh and replenish
Stalk-eaten tops,
Until the next time
The cattle pass through.

Does the stream
Sing Your name, Jesus?
Do the hills
Praise You?
I strain to listen for their melody,
But it is heard only by ears
More sensitive than mine.

In this place there is no fear.
Only the encompassing arms of
The Lord Jesus Christ and His love.

The Lord is gracious and merciful,
Slow to anger and great in lovingkindness.
The Lord is good to all
And His mercies are over all His works.

Psalm 145: 8-9

Your Presence

I feel your presence here.
In the light splashing through the trees,
Playing on the water,
In the song composed by the river gurgle.

Such wonder, inexpressible.
Yet I do try and express
The warmth
The love
The light.
The stillness of a voice
Breathed between the tree trunks.
The call of a bird
High in the air.
The small cloud shimmering,
White overhead.

A voice that speaks worlds, energy
Into existence.
I feel you all around me,
Rejoicing.
I sit in the middle of your goodness,
Light playing and dappling
across the colours of the grass

Beneath old totara trees.
Light producing endless patterns
Never to be repeated.

I walked into a room once
The main living area of a house.
It was all golden and shimmering
Decorated with gilded mirrors and golden clocks.
The golden frames of paintings
Hung on gold wallpaper.
I understood this,
A small rendition of the king's palace
Here on earth.

For me,
This tree grove is my glimpse of that place,
My glimpse of the eternal.
The singing river
Playing, meandering through a green landscape,
Green grass hills and ever-green totaras.
A place of peace, of calm,
Of the Lord God's presence.

It is in this place with its playful stream
And stately totara trunks
Lit with a back light of gold
That I meet with You, my Lord.

More than Pretty

I want more than pretty.
I long to express
A beauty
Far beyond this realm.
Something that reflects
The glory and holiness
Of our Lord God.

How can I do this?
To what place shall I go?
The Bible, the love letter of God.
People meeting with the Lord,
His train filling the temple,
And all the angels
Bow down
And cry
Holy.

His beauty is expressed
In a reaction
As well as one word.

Holy!

All Thy works shall give thanks to Thee, O Lord.
And Thy godly ones shall bless Thee.
They shall speak of the glory of Thy kingdom
And talk of Thy power;

Psalm 145: 10-11

Thin Place

In the thin place,
We can take the hand of Jesus,
And the veil between
Eternity and time
Easily parts.
Then a person may step through
Into the presence
Of the Lord God.

Here rainbows of promise
And delight,
Lift up the heart.

To make known to the sons of men
Thy mighty acts,
And the glory of the majesty of Thy kingdom.
Thy kingdom is an everlasting kingdom,
And Thy dominion endures throughout all generations.

Psalm 145: 12-1

My Heart

My heart is full
Of a never-ending song.
The strings of my being
Sing for joy
To the everlasting God.
My mouth overflows with praise
For the Almighty.

What a day,
Blue, blue, blue, sapphire sky
And stillness.
Even the water
Sings quietly today,
As if not to disturb
Angels reclining around the rocks.
A lone cicada
Sings descants
To my own impromptu song.

Fullness of joy
Fullness of love,
Everlasting.

The Lord sustains all who fall,
And raises up all who are bowed down.
The eyes of all look to Thee,
And Thou dost give them
Their food in due time.
Psalm 145: 14-15

Let Our Hands Reach Out.

Let our hands reach out
and touch the face of God.
Let our mouths praise him
From one generation to another.
Let our hearts and words
Encourage one another,
As we tell of the wonder and beauty
Of the living God.
We are fearfully
And wonderfully made;
Each one of us
A special gift created by Him
For Him.
He is the master potter
We are the clay instrument.
So, let us be His music.
Let praises and thanksgiving
Fill our mouths.
Let us speak against the fortresses
Of the ungodly,
And set the prisoners free.

Thou dost open Thy hand
And dost satisfy the desire of every living thing.
The Lord is righteous in all His ways,
And kind in all His deeds.
Psalm 145: 16-17

First Love

You are my first love.

My mind reaches out to find you,

Past the sound of rain on the window,

The music on the stereo,

A room full of paintings.

You meet me here,

Beyond and above all,

Always, my first love.

I close my eyes

And feel Your presence.

I breathe you in, deeply,

As a wonderful perfume.

I desire you to flood my being

Totally.

I want to stay in this place

Where Your face shines upon me.

Where I praise You,

Praise You.

Waterfall words fall from my lips,

Finishing with

Amen.

I love You and extol You, Lord Jesus.

The Lord is near to all who call upon Him,
To all who call upon Him in truth.
He will fulfil the desire of those who fear Him,
He will also hear their cry and will save them.
Psalm 145: 18-19

Kiss of Air

A gentle kiss of air brushed
Past my lips
As I finished my lone song of praise
To You, my God.
How I adore and love You,
Holy, holy Lord.
Let me delight in You,
Be a shining star
Burning bright for You.
How I long for You.
Help me live my life to please You,
Lord God, my Jesus.

There is a place
Sitting at the feet of Jesus.
The place that Mary chose.
A place of closeness,
A place to hear
The words spoken from heaven.

The Lord keeps all who love Him,
But all the wicked, He will destroy.
My mouth will speak the praise of the Lord
And all flesh will bless His holy name
Forever and ever.
Psalm 145: 20-21

A Place of Wonder

Let us sit

And ponder,

In the place of wonder.

Where burdens are light

And joy is a wisp

Floating all around us.

Ethereal spirit

Outpoured,

Part of the presence of the eternal Saviour.

I sit in this place

Of cascading goodness,

And feel it

Falling, falling,

Then filling, filling,

Rushing over me,

Bubbling over,

A joy without limits

Uncaptured,

Free.

But now I find, we sit in a new reality

Of post democracy,

Of covid mandates and vaccinations.

Is this the pouring out
Of the first bowl
of the wrath of God?

Whatever it is,
Whatever may come,
I am held in a bubble,
Protected and loved
By my Lord God.

I Will Praise You

I will praise You, Lord of Lords
And King of Kings.
Your peace comes into my heart
In this quiet place
Where the kingfisher calls,
And I hear the song of the tui.
A grey warbler trills
To the first of the summer cicadas
That sing a lone chorus
Next to the ever-bubbling water.

I plunge
Into cool, forest green liquid.
The heat of the day
Leaves my body.
Now, I can leave this ancient place
And return to the house on the hill.
A place where its own history
Meets technology,
And I will once again, engage
With the news of the world.

Tiny ripples
Distort the reflection
Of a filigree of ferns
Overhanging the water.
The mirror of life is distorted,
But one day we will see
Our Creator
Face to face.

Poem inspired by Psalm 118

From the narrow place of my distress
I called upon the Lord.
The Lord answered me
And set me in a large land.

The Lord heard my prayers
And now I gaze out a
Wide, wide window
Over green, molded hills
Wet from a morning fog.
A large place,
Shimmering.
The Lord is my strength
And song,
He is my salvation.
The blue of a kingfisher
Flashes by.
The blue of a kingfisher
Finds its way
Into my painting.
I give thanks to the Lord
For He is everlasting.
I give thanks to the Lord
For it is He who is my song.

How lovely are Thy dwelling places,
O Lord of hosts.
My soul longed and even yearned for the courts of the Lord;
My heart and my flesh sing for joy to the living God.

Psalm 84: 1-2

A Dark Place

I find myself in a space
Overtaken by darkness.
I run, and come to Your word
Where I wash myself.
Your word cleans me,
Your word fills me,
And sets me free.
Your word brings me joy.

And now the darkness is broken.
I can walk forth
And face the world
Surrounded by Your love,
Protected by Your shield.

I cross the river
And enter Your valley of righteousness.
A place of high hills
And soft warm winds.

Your presence greets me.
I place my hand in Yours.
You draw me in
And we walk together.

The bird also has found a house,
And the swallow a nest for herself, where she may lay her young.
Even Thine altars, O Lord of hosts,
My King and my God.

Psalm 84: 3

Light

Watching the light
Shine on this beauty
Of mixed green nature;
I long to fly home
To where there is no dark
Only eternal day.
I long to explore and enjoy
And hold hands
With the goodness and graciousness
of the Lord God, my Creator.
In His place,
I can soar up the side of a cliff
And expend no energy at all,
Just enjoy the experience.
In His world,
I could grow larger or smaller
And change the perspective
Of what I see
And always be delighted.

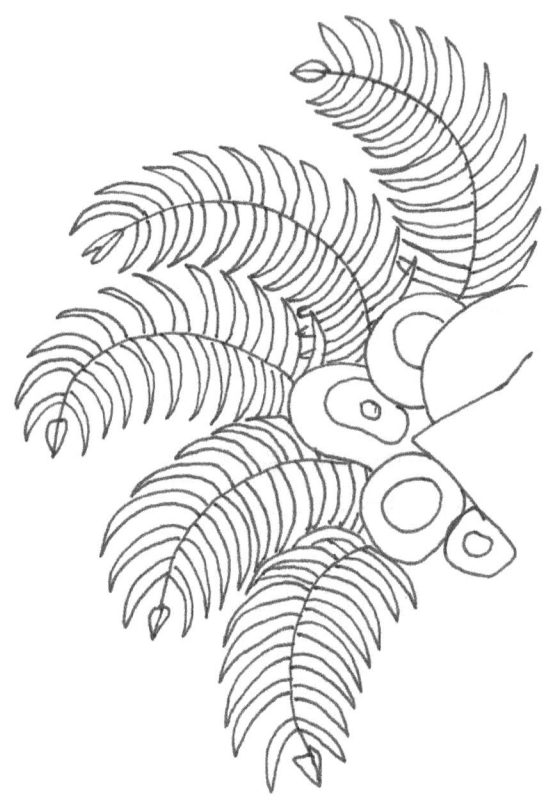

How blessed are those who dwell in Thy house.
They are ever praising Thee.
How blessed is the man whose strength is in Thee;
In whose heart are the highways to Zion.

Psalm 84: 4-5

Storms and Battles

Storms may brew and break overhead,
Battles may rage around me.
Yet this is Your fight
Oh, Lord my God.
I will step back and watch
As You win the battle.
You speak the words of peace
That calm the storm,
Calm the mind,
And calm the soul.

Passing through the valley of Baca, they make it a spring,
The early rain also covers it with blessings.
They go from strength to strength,
Every one of them appears before God in Zion.

Psalm, 84: 6-7

Soaring

My spirit longs to soar
Above hills over-ripe
And kissed hard by a summer sun
That leave multi-folded dents
In a sky
Blue with yearning,
As it stretches towards heaven.

One day
My wing-fettered spirit
Will shake off its shackles
And spread wide,
Flying upward, heavenward.

I won't enter the mouth gaping wide,
The last chute,
The darkened passageway,
Ready to catch
The unwitting crowd.
I have met a Saviour
Who touches my wings,
And sets them free.
Who takes my hand in His,
As together we fly.

O Lord God of hosts, hear my prayer;
Give ear, O God of Jacob
Behold our shield, O God,
And look upon the face of Thine anointed

Psalm 84: 8-9

__Wide Place__

The Lord has set me
In a wide place,
And so, I will sing and proclaim
His praise, His wonder.
He places us in a never-ending story,
Running beyond time.
The Curator of a billion different
Galaxies,
Loves us,
Cares for us,
And takes notice of us.
He fills us with joy.

Open the mouth of your hearts wide
And drink in the sweetness
Of the Lord.
Taste and see,
He is good, He is goodness,
He is our fellowship.
I will follow Him,
My God, forever.

For a day in Thy courts is better than a thousand outside.
I would rather stand at the threshold of the house of my God,
Than dwell in the tents of wickedness.

Psalm 84: 10

The Veil

The veil was so thin, today,
Up there in Holding Paddock.
The heat poured out of the earth
Like waves of God's love,
Inviting me to sit
And deliberate.
But I couldn't,
The call of other commitments
Pushed me on.

I leave that place with a promise.
I will return,
And seek the way through
To meet with my Lord
On the other side of the curtain.

As I go,
I feel the wonder,
The washing of God's love
Through my being.

For the Lord God is a sun and shield;
The Lord gives grace and glory;
No good thing does He withhold from those who walk uprightly.
O Lord of hosts,
How blessed is the man who trusts in Thee.

Psalm 84: 11-12

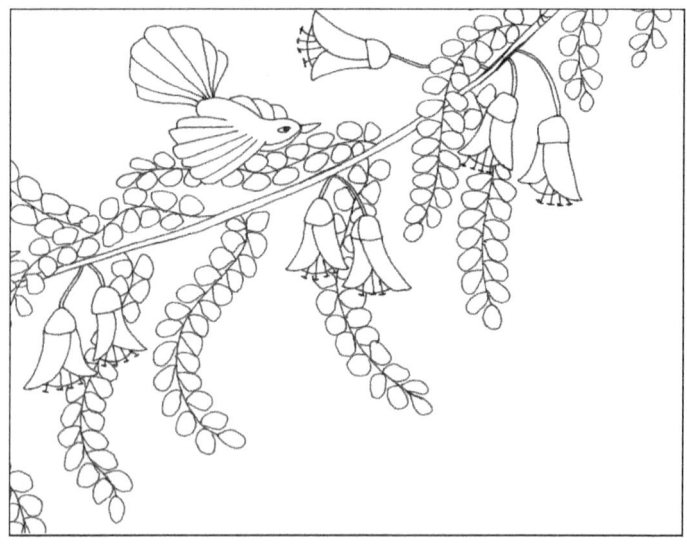

A Place of Rolling Hills

Stretch out the tent cords
Of your future,
And expect to inherit an extensive place.

The Lord has led me
To a broad land.
A place of rolling hills
Trailing upward into green-grey mountains
That cut the sky.
Bush laden.

The Lord has situated me
In a place of singing valleys,
And joyful streams.
A place of goodness
Given from His heart.

The Lord has adopted us
Into a vast kingdom.
Leading on into the enormity
Of eternity;
Of angel choirs and endless music,
And joy.
A place beyond the veil,

The Holy of Holies.
Where we can kneel
Before Him,
And find peace.
The Lord has placed us
In His outstretched hand.

Touched

How can I express
The love that flows from You
Through my being
Then back to You in praise?
How can I express
The fullness of love
That floods me, cascades within me?
The beauty
That a touch from you, Lord God,
May bring.
Of joy tumbling, within and without
Now, rushing over me as a powerful river.
So, I am drenched
By mighty waters of love.
You are my life, my sustenance.
You are my blessing,
You bless me.

The Lord touched me this morning.
His joy ran over my being
Like tiny droplets of water
Falling from the tips of His fingers.
It won't be so long
And we will see him, face to face.

I will give Thee thanks with all my heart;
I will sing praises to Thee before the gods.
I will bow down toward Thy holy temple;
And give thanks to Thy name for Thy lovingkindness and Thy truth;
For Thou hast magnified Thy word according to all Thy name.

Psalm 138: 1-2

Camp Fire

Friends, bleary-eyed
From various qualities of sleep,
Gather around warming flames
And a boiling kettle.
Sunshine filters through
The many branches of
The big old totara tree.
The light reveals columns of smoke
Rising off the breakfast fire.
Forming patterns,
Like the shafts of light
Streaming through stained glass windows
In a church.
And I find
I sit in a place of worship
In the wilderness.

On the day I called Thou didst answer me;
Thou didst make me bold with strength in my soul.
All the kings of the earth will give thanks to Thee, O Lord,
When they have heard the words of Thy mouth.

Psalm 138: 3-4

Taste of Heaven

I discover

A taste of heaven

In colour.

A searching,

A longing

To recreate that lost garden,

Either in paint,

Or in the soil

Outside the old farmhouse.

It doesn't matter which.

I am driven

By a desire

For my true home,

My true love.

And they will sing of the ways of the Lord.
For great is the glory of the Lord.
For though the Lord is exalted,
Yet He regards the lowly;
But the haughty He knows from afar.

Psalm 138: 6-7

Your Love, Whispered

I love you, Lord Jesus
I hear You whisper on the wind,
And feel Your love
Wrap around me
In the perfume of the garden roses,
In the colours of Your creation.

You dwell in the heights.
You dwell in my praises.
I listen
And in the rustle of the leaves
Of the magnolia tree,
I hear Your love spoken.

I feel gentle breeze kisses
On the side of my face
As You pass by, caressing.
I meet with You here,
And Your love,
Your presence
Surrounds me,
Always.

Though I walk in the midst of trouble, Thou wilt revive me;
Thou wilt stretch forth Thy hand against the wrath of my enemies,
And Thy right hand will save me.
The Lord will accomplish what concerns me;
Thy lovingkindness, O Lord, is everlasting;
Do not forsake the works of Thy hands.

Psalm 138: 7-8

Floating in the Words of a Psalm

I float,
Immersed in the words of a psalm.

The presence of the Lord
Blows in as a wind,
Holding me, supporting me on a breath.

I meditate on the goodness
That pours forth from Your word.
Your love wraps around me
In such a way,
I must catch my spirit,
As immortality longs to
Burst forth from this earthly shell
Of mortality,
And follow You into the eternal.

This vessel
Cannot contain the joy
That You pour into me
And around me.
It spills over, splashing about my being.
So that I long to be free
And fly away with You,

But this is not my time.

You are my life, my love,
You fill me.
Then You take me soaring
Over the heights.

Sit at the Feet of Jesus

Enter the place of marvel
Where the air is clear
And full of singing.
Where earthly ideas
Fade into the distance
As we meet with
The Living God.

This is the place to contemplate
At the feet of Jesus,
The place to consider
And explore,
Dimensions, universes
The worlds under His care.
To discover the Creator
As our Creator.
To enter in
And embrace the fullness of joy.
A place to fill our being
With the contentment of peace.

Let us take His hand
And walk under His wings.

Praise the Lord.

For it is good to sing praises to our God;

For it is pleasant and praise is becoming.

The Lord builds up Jerusalem;

He gathers the outcasts of Israel.

Psalm 147: 1-2

Even in Winter

Even in winter,
When the trees are bare,
And life seems to have curled into a ball
By the fire,
Awaiting spring.
Even in the times of waiting,
Of dullness
Of not much happening,
Of dry desert spirit,
I will choose to praise You,
My Lord, and God.

I will praise You
Every day of my life,
In the times of plenty
and the times of want.
In every circumstance,
I find Your blessing.

I am grateful.

He heals the broken hearted,
 And binds up their wounds.
He counts the number of the stars;
He gives names to all of them.

Psalm 147: 3-4

A Hiding place

Take your place
at the feet of Jesus.
Where all sound of the world,
Both rural and city,
Fade.
Here, we discover the words
Of our Creator,
The living Spirit
That gives us life.

There is a place
Hidden in the cleft of the rock.
A room so small
No bigger than a cupboard.
Where we may cry out to
Our Saviour.
He will draw near,
Pass by,
That we may live.

These are places not to be neglected,
To be visited often.
Places of refreshing,
Of abundant joy and gladness.

Great is our Lord, and abundant in strength;
His understanding is infinite.
The Lord supports the afflicted;
He brings down the wicked to the ground.
Psalm 147: 5-6

Sing in the Hills

We sing in the hills
Where our wind-torn voices
Are whipped away,
Taken by the edge of a stiff breeze.
Our words,
Are cast out beyond us,
Thrown around
The hills and valleys.
Maybe never heard
By another human,
Or only caught
On the edge of hearing
By some passing traveller.

The Lord Hears,
He enjoys our delight.
And He,
In return,
Rejoices over us with His song.

Sing to the Lord with thanksgiving;
Sing praises to our God on the lyre,
Who covers the heavens with clouds,
Who provides rain for the earth,
Who makes grass to grow on the mountains.

Psalm 147: 7-8

You Are here

You are here
In the busy-ness of the city,
In the hum of the morning traffic,
In the smell of a thousand homes
Preparing breakfast.

You are here,
Walking among one million people,
Sitting beside hundreds of commuters,
Travelling on the many buses and trains,
Of the city.
Your Spirit
Hovers over the vastness of buildings
Rising tall,
Sprawled across the land.
You see each one of us.

You are here
In the hush of a room
Surrounded by noise.
Into the tiniest of quiet spaces,
You come
And meet with us.

He gives to the beast its food,
And to the young ravens which cry.
He does not delight in the strength of the horse;
He does not take pleasure in the legs of a man.

Psalm 147: 10-11

Can I Praise You?

Can I praise You
Under the dullness
Of a grey sky?
Or in the bleakness of life?
At a time when the future is unclear?
Can I praise You
As the south wind, bitter,
Bites at my legs,
And my hands go numb,
Even as I shove them into my pockets?

Yet, in all these things,
I feel the fullness of Your Presence,
The beauty of Your joy.
I do have the will to praise You.
In the good and the bad,
I choose to praise You,
To thank You.
I praise You, Jesus,
I join in with the cry of the gull,
And the crashing of the sea
On a cold autumn sand.
In all things, I praise You.
Jesus, my Lord.

The Lord favours those who fear Him,
Those who wait for His lovingkindness.
Praise the Lord, O Jerusalem.
Praise your God, O Zion.

Psalm 147: 11-12

A Painted Sky

The Lord gave me a painted sky
Today.
I know it wasn't just for me,
But He and I enjoyed it.

Two pathways of shelf cloud
Cut across the blue;
And pepperings of small rounded cream-puff clouds,
In various shades of purple and greys
Floated up,
Out of the distant horizon,
Like stepping stones to heaven.

I wonder if angels
Sat on the various levels of white
Above me?

High cirrus
Formed maceral judder bars,
Heralding in, a coming front of rain.
But not for today.

In the meantime,
I sit on a log

And enjoy the rolling of the surf.
I watch black-backed gulls
Drop pipi shells from a height,
Breaking them open.
While I relax
In the beauty of the beach.

At the End

I stand on
The end of a bridge,
And gaze out
To a far distant land,
Hidden beyond the horizon.

There is a place,
A day coming,
When we will roam over hills
That shout and echo with joy.
Where flowers sing
And the pathways are paved in gold.
Where streams of living water,
Flow;
And the righteous shall dance in delight.
There is a place of warm winds
Blowing,
Playing, laughing.
Where our lives are upheld
With the ever-present breath
Of our Lord God.

About the Author:

When I was a child
I knew the love of the Lord God.
He surrounded me and protected me.
When I was young, I asked Jesus to be my Saviour.

When I was a teenager,
I did not follow His precepts.
I did not understand
That in them was life,
In them was joy.
The pull and drag of the world
Took me
Into ungodly and unsatisfying ways.

When I became an adult,
Jesus met with me.
"Follow Me and forsake other paths,
Find joy, contentment and peace with Me."
How could I turn away from such a great love?
I chose to follow Him.

But life is a battle,
Our enemy, Satan is out to cheat, steal and destroy.
Although I stumbled,
I did not fall.

Jesus always rescued me from any miry pit.
He longs to do the same
For each of us
Who will ask.

Jesus wins my battles.
He has brought me into a wonderful place,
A place of love, joy and contentment.
He surrounds me with beauty
And good people.
I am grateful
Jesus saved me,
And that He blesses me.
Jesus has blessed
He continues to bless
And He will bless
My life,
Forever.

Geraldine Craw 2022

A big thank you to Christel Jeffs for reading and discussing my work.
And thank you to the NZ Christian Writers Group for their encouragement.
Also, thanks to the Whangarei Poetry Group who keep poetry alive.

Other Books by Geraldine Craw (Geraldine Paul).

Timothy Tui longs to explore New Zealand, but his short, forest-bird wings don't allow him to fly very far. Timothy and his friends meet three albatrosses. Can they help Timothy? Reading age 8 years+

Francesca Fantail's favourite event of the year is the Wild West Coast Sandfly Festival. But things start to go wrong when Romeo, chef extraordinaire, dies. Can Fran sort things out? Reading age 8 years+

Enjoy colouring the bird trails of fantails and other birds as they hop and fly through the New Zealand bush. Take on the adventure of soaring past waterfalls, making them your own with colour.

Tatena sees visions. She wants to know why. A vision of a great city being attacked by dark, other-world riders, sends Tatena on a journey. Something awful is about to happen. Can she do anything to stop the impending doom? Reading 12+

www.ingramcontent.com/pod-product-compliance
Lightning Source LLC
Chambersburg PA
CBHW060419050426
42449CB00009B/2026